Why Do We Have Seasons?

# WHY IS IT Fall?

## Sara L. Latta

# Enslow Elementary

an imprint of

 **Enslow Publishers, Inc.**
40 Industrial Road
Box 398
Berkeley Heights, NJ 07922
USA

http://www.enslow.com

# Words to Know

**harvest (HAR vest)**—The food gathered at the end of the growing season.

**migrate (MY grate)**—To move from one place to another.

**season (SEE zuhn)**—One of the four parts of the year. Each season has a certain kind of weather.

**tilt**—To lean to one side.

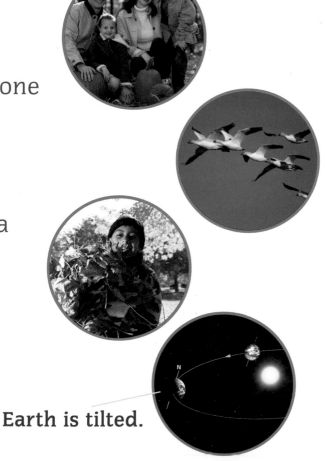

**Earth is tilted.**

# contents

# What is fall?

There are four seasons of the year. Fall is one of the seasons. The others are winter, spring, and summer.

Each season lasts about three months. Each season has its own kind of weather.

winter

spring

summer

fall

Fall is cooler than summer, but warmer than winter.

# Why Do We have seasons?

Earth moves around the sun one time each year. Earth **tilts** as it goes around the sun.

The tilt causes more or less sunlight to fall on different parts of Earth.

Spring in north part of Earth

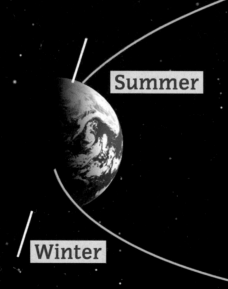

Summer

Winter

North Pole tilts toward the sun; it is summer in the north part of Earth.

Earth's path around sun

North Pole tilts away from sun; it is winter in the north part of Earth.

Winter

Summer

Fall in north part of Earth

As the amount of sunlight changes, the weather changes. So do the seasons.

# When Does fall start?

Fall starts right after summer. In North America, the first day of fall is around September 21. After this day, the days get cooler. The days also get shorter: The sun sets earlier every day.

# Why Do leaves Change Color in fall?

With less sunlight, plants make less food. They get ready to rest for winter. The green part of leaves that makes food goes away.

Now, the leaves show the yellow and orange colors that were hiding behind the green.

# What happens to other plants in fall?

In fall, some plants turn brown and look dead. Their roots are still alive, though. Like the trees, they will rest all winter.

purple coneflower in summer and fall

Many plants make seeds or nuts in the fall. Some of these seeds and nuts will grow into new plants in the spring.

Acorns are oak tree seeds.

13

# What Do animals Do in fall?

In fall, animals get ready for winter. Some grow long, thick fur to keep them warm. Others gather food. Bears eat lots and lots of food in the fall. They will use their fat for energy as they rest over the winter.

**Black Bear**

Busy squirrels store nuts to eat later.

15

# Why Do animals migrate?

Some animals cannot live in the cold winter weather. So in the fall, they migrate to warmer places. Geese and other birds fly south. Many kinds of fish swim to warmer waters.

Monarch butterflies fly thousands of miles to their warm winter homes in Mexico and California.

# What Do People Do in fall?

Many farmers pick their crops in the fall. You may go apple picking or get a Halloween pumpkin. People all around the world celebrate the harvest. In North America, many families share a Thanksgiving feast.

# Do leaves need sunlight to change colors?

You will need:

- 🍁 tree or shrub that turns colors in the fall (ask an adult to help you find one)
- 🍁 heavy paper
- 🍁 masking tape

1. In early fall, find a tree with leaves that you know will turn red or purple. A flowering dogwood tree, a maple tree, or a burning bush would work well.

2. Find some leaves that get plenty of sunlight. (Do not pick them.) Tape a piece of paper to part of each leaf.

3. After the leaves have changed color, remove the pieces of paper. Did the part of the leaf under the paper also turn color? Why or why not?

# Learn More

## Books

Cocca-Lefler, Maryann. *Let It Fall.* New York: Cartwheel Books, 2010.

McKneally, Ranida T. and Lin, Grace. *Our Seasons.* Massachusetts: Perfection Learning, 2007.

Smith, Siân. *Changing Seasons.* Illinois: Heinemann-Raintree, 2009.

# Learn More

## Web Sites

**"Enchanted Learning"**
<http://www.enchantedlearning.com/crafts/fall/>
Creative and enchanting children's crafts for all seasons.

**"Primary Games"**
<http://www.primarygames.com/seasons/seasons.htm>
This web site offers a fun and interactive way to learn the four seasons.

**"Holidays.Kaboose"**
<http://holidays.kaboose.com/fall/>
This web site is filled with winter crafts and recipes for children.

# Index

Enslow Elementary, an imprint of Enslow Publishers, Inc.

Enslow Elementary® is a registered trademark of Enslow Publishers, Inc.

Copyright © 2012 by Sara L. Latta

All rights reserved.

No part of this book may be reproduced by any means without the written permission of the publisher.

Original edition published as *What Happens in Fall* in 1996.

**Library of Congress Cataloging-in-Publication Data**

Latta, Sara L.
  Why is it fall? / Sara L. Latta.
    p. cm. — (Why do we have seasons?)
  Rev. ed. of: What happens in fall? 2006.
  Includes index.
  ISBN 978-0-7660-3985-8
  1. Autumn—Juvenile literature. 2. Seasons—Juvenile literature.
  I. Latta, Sara L. What happens in fall? II. Title.
  QB637.7.L38 2012
  508.2—dc23                    2011019296

Paperback ISBN 978-1-59845-388-1
ePUB ISBN 978-1-4645-0481-5
PDF ISBN 978-1-4646-0481-2

Printed in the United States of America.

102011 Lake Book Manufacturing, Inc., Melrose Park, IL

10 9 8 7 6 5 4 3 2 1

**To Our Readers:** We have done our best to make sure all Internet addresses in this book were active and appropriate when we went to press. However, the author and the publisher have no control over and assume no liability for the material available on those Internet sites or on other Web sites they may link to. Any comments or suggestions can be sent by e-mail to comments@enslow.com or to the address on the back cover.

♻ Enslow Publishers, Inc., is committed to printing our books on recycled paper. The paper in every book contains 10% to 30% post-consumer waste (PCW). The cover board on the outside of each book contains 100% PCW. Our goal is to do our part to help young people and the environment too!

*Note to Parents and Teachers:* The Why Do We Have Seasons? series supports the National Science Education Standards for K–4 science. The Words to Know section introduces subject-specific vocabulary words, including pronunciation and definitions. Early readers may need help with these new words.

**Photo Credits:** © Corel Corporation, pp. 20–23; Enslow Publishers, Inc. p. 12; Mark Garlick/Science Photo Library, pp. 6–7; © 2011 Photos.com, a division of Getty Images. All rights reserved, pp. 4–5, 8–11, 13–19.

**Cover Photo:** ©2011 Photos.Com, a division of Getty Images. All rights reserved.

*Science Consultant,* Harold Brooks, PhD, NOAA/National Severe Storms Laboratory, Norman, Oklahoma

*Series Literacy Consultant,* Allan A. De Fina, PhD, Past President of the New Jersey Reading Association, Professor, Department of Literacy Education, New Jersey City University